Ladybird

PL

CONTENTS

THE ORIGINS OF PLANTS

Plants first appeared on Earth about 630 million years ago, long before animals came into existence. The earliest plants developed in water. Then, around 400 million years ago, vegetation began to grow on land.

Cycads

These ancient plants, which look like a cross between ferns and trees, were already present on Earth over 200 million years ago, at the time of the dinosaurs. Cycads grow from seeds, which can be as large as a hen's egg.

Algae

The first plants were very small and simple. They were similar to **algae**, being made up of single cells. Algae can adapt and grow almost anywhere on Earth where there is moisture.

Giant Sequoias

These trees are among the largest plants in the world. They can grow to over 260 feet tall. They grow mainly in forests along the North American Pacific Coast. People have cut tunnels through sequoia trunks that are wide enough to drive a car through.

WHAT ARE PLANTS?

Plants are life forms that have hard cell walls and produce their own food by **photosynthesis**. There are over 275,000 different kinds of plants in the world today. The most important plants are the seed producers: flowering plants and conifers.

Chlorophyll
This is the substance in leaves that makes them green. It also helps to make the plant's food through photosynthesis.

Flowers
Flowers contain sweet nectar that attracts insects.

Stem
The stem supports the rest of the plant.

Leaves
Most of a plant's chlorophyll is stored in its leaves.

Photosynthesis
Chlorophyll makes the plant's food in the leaves by combining carbon dioxide from the air, hydrogren from water, and energy from the sun.

Roots
The roots take water and minerals from the soil.

Flowering Plants

Flowers attract animals (insects, bats, birds) to **pollinate** them. **Fruits** develop from pollinated flowers, and **seeds** develop in fruits. When seeds mature and start to grow, called **germination**, new plants are produced.

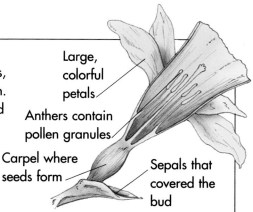

Large, colorful petals

Anthers contain pollen granules

Carpel where seeds form

Sepals that covered the bud

Parasitic Plants

Mistletoe is a parasite. It grows on the branches of trees like apple and poplar. It uses its roots to reach the tree's **xylem**, drawing off water and mineral salts from the tree rather than from the soil.

Epiphytes

Epiphytes grow on the sides of other plants, obtaining mineral salts from rain instead of soil. A bromeliad is a kind of epiphyte whose leaves form a cup at its center. The cup fills up when it rains, providing the plant with water. The plant also "digests" insects and other debris that fall in.

Fungi

Mushrooms and toadstools—also called fungi—are not true plants. Because they have no chlorophyll, they cannot produce food by photosynthesis. Instead, they feed on rotting vegetation.

7

THE WORLD'S FORESTS

Almost three-quarters of the Earth's land is covered with trees. They form forests that are home to many other plants and animals. Although trees exist in a wide range of **habitats**, some parts of the world, such as the polar regions or deserts, are too cold or dry for trees to survive.

Tropical Rain Forests
The hot, humid climate of regions near the Equator support tropical rain forests. In just one square mile of rain forest, there may be 300 different types of tree.

Deciduous Forests

Deciduous trees shed their leaves in autumn, and then grow new ones in spring. Deciduous forests grow where there are distinct seasons, and the weather becomes colder during the winter.

Coniferous Forests

Conifers grow in cold, dry climates. Their leaves are needle-shaped, allowing snow to fall off them more easily. Most conifers do not lose all their leaves at once, but shed them continuously throughout the year.

SURVIVAL IN THE HEAT

The sun's burning heat, freezing temperatures at night, and lack of rain create the desert, an environment too harsh for most plants. But cacti and other **succulents** have **evolved** to survive in these conditions. Other plants spring into life in the sandy soil when it rains.

Lack of Leaves

Cacti have spines rather than leaves. These reduce the amount of water lost by **transpiration**. They also protect the plants against animals that might otherwise eat the cacti.

Under the Ground

Cacti roots are often shallow and extend over a wide area. This helps them to absorb dew, the moisture that forms in the early morning.

10

The Effect of Rain

There is no regular rainfall in the desert. Some places stay dry for many years. But when the rain finally falls, seeds that have been lying in the sandy soil since the last rain germinate.

They quickly produce plants, then flowers, then fruits, then more seeds, which survive until the next rain. Meanwhile, for a short time, the desert landscape is transformed into a mass of color.

Long-lived Survivors

Succulents grow in the desert. They have thick, fleshy leaves where they store water. These desert plants grow slowly—some can live for well over 100 years. If pieces of cacti or other succulents break off, they can take root in the desert sand and grow into new plants.

SURVIVAL IN THE COLD

The ground is permanently frozen in cold northern parts of the world. During the very short summers, the top layer of soil thaws and the ground becomes marshy. Trees cannot grow because of the frozen ground and cold summers, and the landscape looks bleak. There may be a few willow or alder bushes, and small flowering shrubs. The ground is covered with low-growing grasses, mosses, herbs, and lichens.

Lichens

Lichens are the most common form of plant life in the polar regions, the Arctic and Antarctica—the coldest places on Earth.

Lichens grow very slowly. They are surprisingly colorful, often displaying shades of pink or red.

Arctic Flowers

In polar regions, flowering plants grow close to the ground, their blooms sheltered from fierce winds. Annuals—plants that flower and die in a year—are very rare in cold climates, because they cannot produce seeds before the snow buries them.

True Partnership

Lichens are a combination of algae and fungi. The algae, which contain chlorophyll, photosynthesize and produce food, while the fungi provide minerals and protective housing for the more fragile algae. The partnership allows both plants to survive. It is called **symbiosis.**

Arctic Diet

Plant-eating animals such as reindeer and Arctic hares depend on tiny plant life to survive in the cold Arctic environment.

ENJOYING THE WATER

Some plants live entirely underwater. Others have underwater roots, but their leaves and flowers are above the surface. The roots of many water plants act as anchors. Water-plant leaves are often long and thin or feathery.

Giant Water Lily
This plant grows in the Amazon River in South America. Its leaves can grow to be as wide as a bus and are strong enough to support the weight of a sitting child.

Pond Plants
Different plants grow at different depths in water.

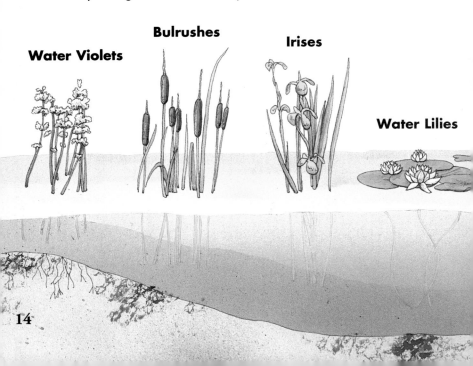

Water Violets

Bulrushes

Irises

Water Lilies

Mangrove Swamps

Found in marshy areas near the sea, mangrove trees grow in salty water. Some of their roots grow up out of the mud, to take oxygen from the air at low tide.

Coastal Scene

Grasses often grow in sand leading down to the seashore. They produce stems called **rhizomes** that burrow down into the sand and anchor the grasses against the wind. Once the sand is firm, flowering plants that can live in the salty environment will start to grow. On the rocks, seaweeds (a form of algae) cling fast as the tide moves in and out.

THE MEAT-EATERS

In parts of the world where the soil is boggy and has a low mineral content, meat-eating plants have evolved. Enticing scents and sweet nectar lure insects—or in some cases, small mammals—to fall into highly specialized traps. When captured, their remains are slowly digested by the plant.

Venus's-flytrap

Found in the swamplands of North and South Carolina in the U.S., the scent of this plant attracts flies to its open leaves. In the center of the leaves are special trigger spikes. When an insect brushes against the spikes, the leaves spring shut in a fraction of a second, trapping the insect inside.

Sarracenia

The sarracenia is like a hollow tube. Flies and other insects crawl onto the rim of the plant. They lose their grip and tumble down inside, unable to escape.

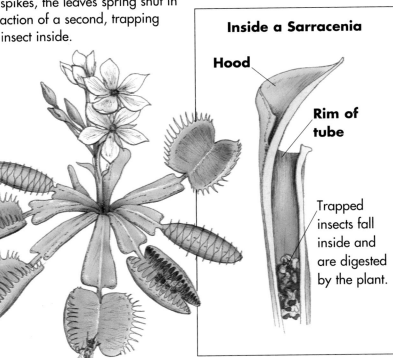

Inside a Sarracenia

Hood

Rim of tube

Trapped insects fall inside and are digested by the plant.

Sundews

This group of plants grows throughout the world. Their sticky appearance lures insects down onto their leaves.

But once a fly lands here, it will be unable to escape. It dies, and its body is slowly digested by the plant.

Pitcher Plants

These plants come in many different shapes and sizes. They may fill up with rainwater. Some pitcher plants may grow to a height of 120 feet by climbing up trees, whereas others stay much closer to the ground.

A SILVER FIR TREE

A silver fir tree, like most conifers, does not change through the year. It keeps its green coloration year round. Conifers are most common in colder parts of the world. They grow taller than any other trees. A redwood in the Redwood National Park in California is the tallest tree on Earth. It measures over 330 feet tall—taller than eighteen giraffes! Conifers also live longer than most other trees. Bristlecone pine trees could live for up to 5,500 years.

Plantations

Conifers are grown commercially in plantations both as a source of timber and for the paper industry. They are also grown as Christmas trees, a fashion started in England by Queen Victoria's husband, Prince Albert, in the 19th century.

Needles

The leaves of a conifer are shaped like needles. Most conifers do not lose their needles in the fall, but shed and replace them gradually all year long.

Cones

Pinecones come in different shapes and sizes. When they are ripe and the weather is warm, they open up and the seeds drop out. Squirrels and some birds feed on pinecones.

Cone

Seeds

A HORSE CHESTNUT TREE

As the seasons change through the year, a horse chestnut tree changes, too. In the autumn, the leaves lose their green color. Growth and photosynthesis both stop, as the weather becomes colder. The link between the leaves and branches weakens and the tree loses its leaves, especially in windy weather. In time, the leaves will rot in the ground and release valuable nutrients into the soil, which the tree may take up again through its roots. The tree is dormant over the winter, before growing new leaves again in the spring.

Seeds

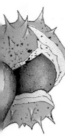

The spiky seed capsule of the horse chestnut splits apart when it hits the ground. There may be one to three seeds inside. Some are round in shape, while others can have flat sides.

Seedling

Left lying on the surface of the soil, the seed starts to germinate, a root and shoot growing through its outer covering.

Sapling

At this stage, the small tree is called a sapling. It is vulnerable to trampling feet and grazing animals. But if it survives, a horse chestnut tree may live more than 150 years.

Leaf

Horse chestnut trees have compound leaves, which are made up of a number of leaflets.

Scale

The base of a horse chestnut may be wider than a truck. It can grow as tall as a ten-story building.

Trunk Segment

The age of a tree can be determined by counting the growth rings in its trunk. It is also possible to see how much a tree grew in a particular year, and when it had to survive tough conditions, such as a forest fire. This study of a tree's growth rings is called **dendrochronology**.

Bark

The tough, protective covering on the outside of the tree has minute holes in it, known as lenticels, through which gases can move in and out of the tree's stem.

Cork cambium from which the bark develops

Snowproof Shape

The downward, triangular shape of many conifers allows snow to fall off them easily. Otherwise, the weight of accumulating snow could break off their branches.

Roots

The roots anchor the tree in the ground and provide it with a way to get nutrients from the soil. The roots of some conifers spread out a considerable distance from the tree itself.

Life Cycle of a Horse Chestnut Tree

Spring

In the Northern Hemisphere, leaves start to appear in late March or early April.

Summer

The leaves are heavy and green. Fruits have smooth outer casings.

Autumn

The leaves turn yellow and fall off. The now spiky fruits also fall to the ground.

Winter

The tree has now lost all of its leaves. Sticky winter buds form at the ends of its branches.

GROWING AND SPREADING

Many flowering plants use seeds to reproduce. Some plants can also divide from their roots, stems, buds, or leaves to reproduce. This is called **vegetative reproduction**. It allows plants to spread more rapidly than is possible from seed.

Bulbs

An onion is a bulb. If you slice it in half, you will see it is made up of tightly packed leaves. Roots grow out from the base of the bulb, with new bulbs developing on the sides. A bulb is actually a type of bud.

Tubers

Some plants, like potatoes, have underground stems that swell at their ends to form **tubers**.
If you look closely at a potato, you can see the scar where it was attached to a stem as it grew underground.

Epiphytic Orchids

These plants use their roots to anchor themselves to a tree.

THE FLOWERING CYCLE

For a seed to form, pollen from the male part of the plant must reach the female part. When this happens within the same plant, it is called self-pollination. More often, cross-pollination occurs—two plants are involved. Insects and other creatures, such as nectar-feeding birds, transfer pollen as they fly between flowers. Pollen is visible on the **stamen** inside the flower—it looks like powder.

Wind Pollination

Some plants such as grasses and many kinds of tree depend on the wind rather than insects for pollination. Their flowers are very small and they have no nectar. Produced in huge quantities, the pollen granules are very light and are carried from plant to plant by air currents. Many people are allergic to this type of pollen, and suffer from hay fever as a result.

Insect Pollination

Many flowers have colored petals that attract insects. When an insect comes to feed on the flower's nectar, it brushes against the male anther, collecting pollen. When the insect lands on another flower of the same species, it rubs this pollen onto the female **stigma**. In this way, pollination occurs.

Sycamore Seeds

Sycamore Leaves

Oak Leaves

Pine Needles

Seed Dispersal

Sycamore seeds form in capsules that are carried long distances by the wind. Pinecones spill their seeds onto the soil. While storing food for winter, squirrels carry acorns away from the oak tree to places where they may grow.

Acorns

Pinecones

Sea Travel

Coconut palms growing near the sea may drop their fruits—coconuts—into the water. The coconuts are carried away to distant shores, where they can grow into new trees.

Helpful Birds

Birds that eat fruits such as berries also spread seeds. Although the bird's stomach digests the soft part of the fruit, the seeds remain intact. The bird then passes the seeds out in its droppings, often far away from where it ate the fruit.

27

PROTECTION AND WEAPONS

Because plants cannot protect themselves by running, hiding, or fighting, many species have developed special forms of self-defense. Sharp spines and poisonous berries can help keep hungry herbivores away.

Bramble

Raspberry and blackberry plants grow into prickly shrubs commonly called brambles. The spikes on bramble stems form a thick barrier as the plant grows over a wide area.

Sharp prickles break off like splinters.

Even the leaves have small prickles on their undersides.

Acacias

Acacias grow quickly, protected by thousands of vicious spines. Mature acacias have no lower branches; only the tall giraffe can reach its leaves. The giraffe's long tongue and mouth are not injured by the spines.

Toxic Protection

Poison protects some plants. The entire bitter nightshade plant is poisonous and can be fatal if eaten. Other plants, such as poison ivy and poison oak, transmit poison through external contact.

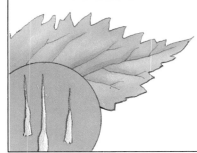

Why Nettles Sting

This close-up picture shows the sharp hairs on a nettle leaf. When touched, the hairs break off and release painful formic acid into the skin, causing a rash. Cutting nettles back regularly strengthens their stinging power.

PLANTS UNDER THREAT

Whole communities of plants are being destroyed every day all over the world, particularly in tropical regions. Huge areas of forest are being cleared to supply timber, often for furniture or firewood. Little is being done to replant these forests. Because the trees take many years to grow, some species are becoming endangered.

Growing Firewood

To help conserve forests, some trees are now being planted especially for the purpose of providing fuel. The neem tree was taken to Ghana in Africa from India in the early 1900s. Today it is widely grown. Bats feeding on its fruits have spread its seeds and helped to establish it over a large area.

Plant "Poaching"

Although plants can be cultivated in nurseries, some, like cacti, are slow to grow and can take many years to reach a large size. They are threatened by people who search for large specimens in the wild and dig them up. There are laws that prohibit the sale of endangered wild plants, but it is difficult to enforce these laws.

Vital Source of Fuel

In many areas, particularly in developing countries, trees are vital as the only available fuel. People still need wood for cooking and heating.

BREEDING PLANTS

People have been breeding plants for centuries. This has led to a wide range of cultivated crops and plants that are raised on farms and in gardens and homes. Scientists develop **strains** that are more resistant to disease and grow well in harsher conditions. Crossing two or more strains produces first generation **hybrids**, which are often bigger, stronger, and more fruitful plants than their predecessors.

Decorative Plants
Commercial nurseries test new strains of plants to ensure they will grow well before they are made available to the public. This type of research can take several years. Plant scientists can now alter the colors and sizes of flowers, to increase the variety of plants that can be grown in the house or garden.

Orchid Cultivation

Certain plants are much harder to grow from seed than others. Orchids grow best on a special chemical mix, rather than in soil. The seeds are grown in sealed flasks, where germination may take from a few days to several months. The seedlings remain in the flask for up to a year before being planted in pots.

Cereals—Yields and Costs

Cereal crops—wheat, maize, rice, and others—are important sources of food. High-yield strains have been produced, but they often require special chemical fertilizers and pesticides. Increasingly, farmers have returned to native strains that are hardier and cheaper to grow. International research centers in Mexico and the Philippines store many different kinds of wheat, maize, and rice in seed banks for future use. These are often wild strains; few can be found in their places of origin.

PLANTS HELPING PEOPLE

We depend on plants in many areas of our lives. People use reeds and timber to build homes. Baskets, bags, floor coverings, and other household objects can be woven from plant materials. Plants make up a large part of the foods we eat, in the form of fruits, vegetables, and grains—even the feed for livestock that provide meat. We have much to learn about the medicinal uses of plants as well. Western scientists are now working with rain forest people to learn about the plants they use for healing purposes. The study of plants that are useful to people is called economic botany.

Grains

For thousands of years, people all over the world have grown crops to provide a variety of foods. These range from wheat for making bread to sunflowers for sunflower oil. The crops are cultivated in fields and harvested at the end of the growing season.

Medicines

Many drugs used to treat illnesses contain chemicals obtained from plants. Digitalis, a poisonous substance found in foxgloves, is used to treat some heart patients.

Perfumes

Roses and other fragrant plants contain special oils that can be made into perfumes. A number of these "essential essences" are also used in lotions and ointments that can help people reduce stress.

Insecticides

Plants have developed ways of avoiding attacks by insects. Pyrethrin is a chemical present in a type of flower called a chrysanthemum. It is deadly to insects, but does not cause serious harm to most other creatures. It is now used as an insecticide, a chemical used to kill harmful insects that damage crops.

Clothing and Dyes

For centuries, plant fibers such as cotton and flax have been made into clothes. Some plants, such as woad, produce dyes that are used to color cloth and, in some cultures, for body painting.

35

AMAZING PLANT FACTS

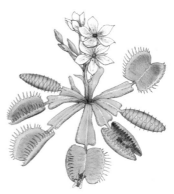

- **Deadly Competition** Guayule plants, which grow in groups in the desert areas of Mexico and Central America, produce an acid from their roots that kills off other vegetation, preventing other plants from growing near them.

- **Drought Resistant** Both the caper plant of the Sahara desert in Africa and the American pygmy cedar can live without taking up any water at all through their roots. They absorb water vapor directly from the air.

- **Under Threat** More than 25,000 of the world's flowering plants—about one-tenth of the total number of plants on the planet—are now in danger of extinction.

- **Tree House** The baobab tree has a huge swollen trunk that is very soft. Native peoples of Africa and Australia have been known to hollow out these trees and make homes inside them.

- **Largest Leaves** The raffia palm, which grows on islands in the Indian Ocean, has leaves up to 60 feet long.

- **Biggest Seed** Found only on the Seychelles Islands off the coast of Africa, the Coco de Mer palm produces huge nuts that can weigh more than forty pounds. There are both male and female forms of this palm. Only the female trees produce these huge nuts, while the male palms produce pollen.

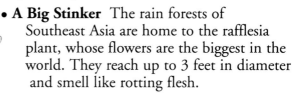

- **A Big Stinker** The rain forests of Southeast Asia are home to the rafflesia plant, whose flowers are the biggest in the world. They reach up to 3 feet in diameter and smell like rotting flesh.

- **Old-timer** A bristlecone pine tree in the White Mountains of California is thought to be around 4,700 years old.

GLOSSARY

Algae Ancient group of simple plants that often grow in water.

Dendrochronology The technique of finding a tree's age by counting the rings in its trunk.

Epiphyte A plant that grows on the branches of another plant and doesn't take root in the soil.

Evolve To change gradually over many years.

Fruit The structure that contains the seeds developing from a pollinated flower.

Germination The process that results in seeds sprouting and growing.

Habitat The area where a plant naturally grows.

Hybrid A plant that is produced by crossing two similar but different plants.

Photosynthesis The process that allows plants to make their food from sunlight.

Pollinate The transfer of pollen to the stigma that fertilizes the flower.

Rhizome An underground stem present in some plants that helps them to spread.

Seed The structure that holds the embryonic plant and stored food developing in a fruit.

Stamen The male part of a flower where pollen is produced.

Stigma The female part of the flower where pollination takes place.

Strain A plant that has been grown under special conditions for a particular purpose.

Succulent A plant that has thick fleshy tissues, such as stems and leaves, that can store water.

Symbiosis A partnership between two life forms that benefits both.

Transpiration Evaporation of water from tiny holes, called pores, in the leaves.

Tuber A short, fleshy underground stem.

Vegetative reproduction The way in which some plants can increase in numbers by growing from existing parts of the plant.

Xylem The system that carries water and mineral salts from the roots to other parts of the plant.

INDEX *(Entries in bold refer to an illustration)*